GOLF LEGENDS

John Daly

Golf Stars of Today

Jack Nicklaus

Greg Norman

Arnold Palmer

Tiger Woods

CHELSEA HOUSE PUBLISHERS

GOLF LEGENDS

JACK NICKLAUS

John Wukovits

CHELSEA HOUSE PUBLISHERS
Philadelphia

Produced by Daniel Bial and Associates
New York, New York

Picture research by Alan Gottlieb
Cover illustration by Bill Vann
Frontispiece photo: Jack Nicklaus

First Printing

1 3 5 7 9 8 6 4 2

Library of Congress Cataloging-in-Publication Data

Wukovits, John F., 1944-
    Jack Nicklaus / by John Wukovits.
        p.   cm. — (Golf legends)
    Includes bibliographical references and index.
    Summary: Traces the career, spanning five decades, of the golf pro
who was named Golfer of the Century in 1988.
        ISBN 0-7910-4560-9 (hc)
    1. Nicklaus, Jack—Juvenile literature.   2. Golfers—United
States—Biography—Juvenile literature.   [1. Nicklaus, Jack.
    2. Golfers.]   I. Title.   II. Series.
    GV964.N5W85   1998
    796.352'092—dc21
    [B]   97-43917
                                                                CIP
                                                                 AC

CONTENTS

1

"AS FINE A ROUND AS I'VE EVER PLAYED"

N o one in the history of golf had so dominated the game like this 46-year-old man had. He was at his best during a tournament's final round, with the championship up for grabs, when he tromped down the fairways like a hungry bear relentlessly pursuing its quarry.

Sixty-nine times in a splendid 22-year professional career, Jack Nicklaus had captured first place, including an incredible 19 victories in the four tournaments called majors—the U. S. Open, the Masters, the British Open, and the PGA Championship—that truly determined whether a player could be labeled great. Only a handful of golfers had won more than two of those coveted titles, and only one other man— the legendary Bobby Jones—had snared more than 10.

Yet few people on this week in April 1986 gave Nicklaus any chance of winning that year's first

Jack Nicklaus blasts out of a sand trap during the second round of the 1986 Masters.

major contest, the Masters. Newspaper reporters wondered in print whether he should step aside from competitive golf and allow younger stars to seize the limelight. Television commentator Ken Venturi, who had enjoyed a successful professional career in the 1960s, bluntly commented that the golfer should "start thinking about when it is time to retire."

Let the critics assail him. He intended to prove that he was not yet over the hill. Taking a pair of scissors out of his drawer, Nicklaus cut out the offending articles and taped them to his refrigerator door as incentives.

"I'm not done, yet," he thought. He had worked hard to improve his game in the weeks immediately prior to the Masters, especially on some of the short shots around the putting greens, called chip shots, which had given him problems recently. He had turned to one of his sons, Jack Jr., who had received lessons in chipping from one of the game's best, fellow golfer Chi Chi Rodriguez. "I had him teach me what Chi Chi had taught him."

Nicklaus approached this tournament with the fierce tenacity that had become one of his trademarks. He wanted to record one more major title, which would both hand him his 20th major and prove that a golfer in his forties could still show the young lions a trick or two.

In fact, when a reporter asked Nicklaus if winning all four major tournaments in one year, a feat that had never been accomplished, was in the back of his mind, he quickly replied, "No, it's in the front of my mind."

Nicklaus posted an unspectacular 74 on Thursday's first round. Then, constantly muttering to himself, "Done, washed up, finished"

Nicklaus celebrates as his putt for birdie drops on the 17th hole at Augusta. The shot capped off his tremendous comeback, giving him the lead and ultimately his sixth Masters title.

as a way of recharging his energy, he followed with a one under par 71 on Friday and a fine 69 on Saturday to put him in ninth place, four shots behind the third round leader, Greg Norman. He would need to pass eight talented golfers and overcome a four-shot deficit if he wanted to win. Though that was not impossible, it was understandable why on Saturday evening no one was talking about Nicklaus's chances of winning. The experts who were thinking about him at all were just impressed that he was in position to finish in the top 10 at his age.

Confidence coursed through his veins as Nicklaus sat down to Saturday dinner with his wife, Barbara, and thought about Sunday's final round. It had long been said that the Masters race does not truly start until the tournament's final nine holes at Augusta National's beautifully sculptured course. The intense pressure from three days of emotion-charged golf combines with the testy back nine to pose a challenge that bests many of the toughest professionals in the game. Especially waiting to trip an unwary player were holes 10 through 13, a series of layouts so formidable that they had earned the nickname Amen Corner, a reference to the sense of relief that gushed out of a player when he completed the four holes without disaster.

Above all, Nicklaus relished a challenge, and he thought he might be ready for Sunday's ordeal. "I think I've found that fellow out there I used to know," he told Barbara to indicate that he was regaining the touch that had propelled him to golf's highest level in the 1960s and 1970s.

Tom Kite, another top professional and who was in front of Nicklaus that Sunday morning, held a different view. Eating his Saturday dinner, Tom Kite summed up the leaders' chances, including Nicklaus's. "I said I not only thought Jack couldn't win this tournament, I said I didn't think he'd ever win another one."

Early Sunday morning, Nicklaus received a telephone call from his second-oldest son, Steve. He wanted to know what score his father might have to shoot to have a chance of winning the Masters. "What do you think, Pop? About a 65 wins it?"

Nicklaus responded, "That's the number I had in mind."

"Then let's go shoot it."

With that encouragement in mind, Nicklaus walked to the first tee along with his caddie, first-born son Jack Nicklaus Jr., called Jackie. Though he knew he had to make a move, nothing seemed to fall into place for him, especially on the fourth and sixth holes where he flubbed relatively easy four-foot putts. By the time he arrived at the ninth tee, he had fallen five shots behind the current leader, Greg Norman. Still, several other golfers had dropped off the pace. Now only two other younger players, Spain's Seve Ballesteros and the United States' Tom Kite, stood between Nicklaus and Norman.

Nicklaus's chances of winning continued to seem extremely remote. Rarely does a golfer come from five shots back with only 10 holes to play in any contest, let alone in the Masters. Nicklaus, though, is not most men, especially in the majors. He thought of nothing but winning, no matter how bad it looked. A bit angry with his lackluster play, he turned to Jackie and muttered, "If I'm going to do anything, I better start doing it."

After a drive and an approach shot placed him 15 feet from the hole, Nicklaus carefully lined up a birdie putt. Suddenly, a colossal roar rose from the gallery watching play at the par-5 eighth green, indicating that one of the leaders had done something spectacular. Pushing the noise from his mind, Nicklaus bent over his putt, but just as he prepared to strike the ball, another tremendous explosion from the eighth gallery shook the course. Both Ballesteros and Kite had holed out

Nicklaus gives an emotional hug to his son, Jack Nicklaus Jr., after winning his record-setting sixth Masters.

their third shots for eagle threes, meaning they shot two strokes under par on the hole.

His predicament worse now, Nicklaus turned to the people watching him and said, "O.K., let's see if we can get a roar up here." The loud laughter not only helped calm the crowd, but also according to Nicklaus "it relaxed me, too." He again bent over the putt, then drilled it directly into the hole for a birdie. The chase was on.

Nicklaus hustled over to the 10th tee, eager for the chance to humble Amen Corner's treacherous holes. If successful, he would place pressure on the leaders following behind, who would still have to play that difficult stretch. When Nicklaus drained birdie putts of 10 feet at the 10th hole and 25 feet at the 11th to pull within two shots of the lead, word spread around the course and brought spectators flooding to the area to see if the old master could pull it off one more time. Even Nicklaus enjoyed the spectacle, claiming later that, "I haven't had this much fun in six years."

A bogey at 12 dropped Nicklaus to three shots back, but instead of letting it bother him, he used the miscue to spur himself on. "It really got me going," he claimed. "I knew I couldn't play defensive with the rest of the course. I knew I needed to be aggressive coming in." A birdie at 13 drew him one shot nearer to the lead. When he walked to the 14th hole, he noticed on a leader board that he trailed only Ballesteros and Kite. Though Nicklaus understood that several golfers were either tied with him or one shot back, "I didn't even look to see who they were. I knew I was going to keep making birdies—or that I had to keep making birdies." He concentrated solely on jumping into the lead, not on who was chasing him.

By now, the gallery following Nicklaus had grown so large that the people in back had trouble seeing over the heads of those in front. The crowd cheered every shot and exploded in delight with each dropped putt. "The noise was deafening," recalled Nicklaus. "I couldn't hear anything. I mean, nothing!"

Nicklaus, who normally showed little emotion on the golf course, fought off tears four or five times over the final five holes because the crowd's tumultuous support so moved him. He had to keep reminding himself: "We have to play golf. This isn't over," and he wondered if he could continue to focus enough to swing his clubs properly. "But I did. One perfect stroke after another." In fact, the sudden onslaught of nerves reminded him of his glory days from earlier years. "When I don't get nervous, I don't make anything."

He must have been terribly nervous on the par-5 15th hole. Two booming shots placed his ball 12 feet from the cup. When he examined the putt, Nicklaus recalled that he had faced the same shot 12 years earlier on this hole and that the ball would not break the way it looked. "It's not what it looks like," he confidently remarked to Jackie moments before sinking the putt for an eagle. He had picked up two strokes on the leaders, but he still remained two shots behind Ballesteros, who had just eagled the par-5 13th hole.

On the 16th, a tortuous par-3 featuring a sloping green and water to the left, Nicklaus drilled a 5-iron that missed going into the hole by inches. He could not see where the ball landed from the tee, but "I could hear the gallery at the green starting to rumble and I said, 'Oops, I've hit it close.'" When he dropped the three-footer for yet another birdie, Nicklaus pulled within one shot of the lead.

The noise level from Nicklaus's gallery rose with each shot. When Nicklaus walked from the 16th green to the 17th tee, hundreds of spectators lined the path, yelling support and slapping his back so frequently that he worried about getting hurt.

As he prepared to hit his tee shot on 17, Nicklaus heard another loud roar from behind, indicating that one of the leaders had done something. "Either Ballesteros holed it or he knocked it in the water," he mumbled to Jackie. After hitting his drive, people in the gallery shouted to Nicklaus that Ballesteros had put his second shot at 15 into the water, giving Nicklaus a share of the lead with the Spaniard and Tom Kite.

Two fine shots placed his ball 15 feet from the cup, but Nicklaus could not determine which way the putt would break. "This putt is impossible to read," he said to his son, so he decided to simply hit the ball straight at the hole. "It wiggled left, wiggled back right and went in the center," he explained later. Nicklaus held the lead with one hole remaining.

The memorable aspect of the 18th hole for Nicklaus was not his score—a routine par four—but the tremendous outpouring of emotion he received from the gallery.

Barely holding back tears as he and his son walked up the final fairway, Nicklaus waved to well-wishers and enjoyed the moment. Jackie later mentioned, "I was getting choked up with all the people cheering on every hole. I was so proud of him."

After his 40-foot birdie putt stopped inches from the hole, Nicklaus tapped in the ball for a par and a record-tying score of 30 for the back nine.

Jackie rushed up, hugged his father, and shouted, "Dad, I loved seeing you play today. It was the thrill of my lifetime. I mean, that was awesome." Father and son then walked arm in arm to the scorer's tent to await the final outcome.

Two golfers still had a chance to win the tournament—Kite and Norman. Kite hit a crisp approach shot to within 12 feet of the hole on 18, but he missed his chance to tie when his birdie putt swerved to the left at the last moment.

That left Greg Norman, who had birdied 17 to move into a tie with Nicklaus. However, he pulled his approach shot into the crowd surrounding

Bernhard Langer, winner of the 1985 Masters, helps Nicklaus put on the traditional green jacket worn by the winner of the Masters.

the 18th green. After a poor chip left him 16 feet from the hole, Norman two-putted for a bogey. At the age of 46, Jack Nicklaus had again won the Masters.

Tom Kite said later, "I hit nearly every shot the way I dreamed about today. But that's the strange thing about golf. You don't have any control about what your opponent does."

What Nicklaus did will long be remembered. In the round's final 10 holes, Nicklaus posted six birdies and one eagle against a solitary bogey—seven strokes under par along a stretch of holes that devour most golfers. In winning his sixth Masters title and 20th major of his splendid career, Nicklaus withstood the stultifying pressure to play as close to a perfect 10 holes as could be done.

"That was as fine a round as I've ever played, especially the last 10 holes," explained a jubilant Nicklaus to reporters after the win. "I've said a hundred times that I'm not as good as I once was. I just want to be occasionally as good as I once was. Today I was."

Maybe he was not as good as he once was, but Nicklaus could still draw upon his legendary golf prowess to hold off the young lions, and in the process remind everybody of how truly talented he was.

2

A KID PLAYING A SPORT

Jack William Nicklaus was born in Columbus, Ohio, on January 21, 1940, to Louis Charles, a drugstore owner, and Nellie Helen Nicklaus. The active youth quickly developed such a talent for causing havoc that his younger sister, Marilyn, labeled him a "great big mischief maker." One time when he was five years old, after watching older boys playing football near his home, young Jack barreled into the house, charged toward the family maid, Annie, and dropped her with a vicious tackle.

Like many boys, Nicklaus played almost every sport available in grade school and junior high school. While he first picked up a golf club at the age of 10, he preferred playing football, basketball, and baseball. "I was having fun," stated Nicklaus. "I was a kid playing a sport. I played all sports; golf was just a sport to me until I was 19 or 20 years old." As a seventh grader, Nick-

Louis Nicklaus gives a pointer to Jack at a local tournament in 1955.

laus played center on the basketball squad, catcher in baseball, and punter and placekicker in football.

He also wanted to be quarterback that year, but his father, also an excellent all-around athlete, claimed Jack was too slow. Rather than give up on the notion, Jack used his father's words as "all the spur I needed." He joined the track team to gain speed, logged a few 11-second 100-yard dashes, and eventually won the quarterback spot.

Nicklaus developed into a fine athlete at Columbus's Upper Arlington High School, where he lettered in four sports—football, baseball, basketball, and golf. Above all, he loved basketball. By his junior year he was averaging 17.5 points per game on offense, and he doggedly pursued his opponents on defense. The next year his prowess on the court earned Nicklaus an honorable mention as an All-Ohio forward.

Nicklaus gradually narrowed his athletic focus until only golf remained. Football lost to golf because their seasons conflicted, and in his senior year he dropped baseball and basketball. While he still loved those sports—even today Nicklaus shoots hoops whenever he can—golf appealed to him because he did not have to rely on others to play. He could grab his clubs and head for the course whenever he wanted. Also, he wanted to excel at something, and as he explained later, "Golf was the only sport at which I could try to become a complete player by myself."

Nicklaus first played golf in 1950 as a 10-year-old. When Louis Nicklaus injured his ankle, the family physician ordered him to walk two hours a day in order to regain strength. Louis took his doctor's order to mean he should go to the golf course regularly, and off to Scioto Country Club in Columbus went the slightly hobbling man and his son. Jack shot a 51 for nine holes the first time he ever played, showing he had a natural talent for the game. He soared to a 60 on the next time out, and so his father enrolled him in the Friday morning golf sessions conducted by Scioto's head professional, Jack Grout.

Grout liked Nicklaus's desire to learn, and he devoted more attention to Jack than to the others. Grout drilled the fundamentals into his pupil, especially balance, keeping his head still during the swing, and hitting down on the ball. Rather than worry too much about direction, Grout ordered Nicklaus to hit the ball as hard and as far as he could. That would not only teach him to drive the ball with power, but it would also stretch his arm muscles. After Jack absorbed these basics, Grout began to work on control and finesse.

Nicklaus picked up the lessons so easily that Grout used him to model shots for the other students in the classes. Rarely did a Friday go by without the other boys and girls hearing Grout bellow, "Jackie, come out here and show us what it means to hit down on the ball" or to demonstrate some other basic principle he was attempting to get across.

Nicklaus's scores plummeted. By the end of that summer, he shot 91 for 18 holes. When he recorded an 81 the following summer, Nicklaus told his dad that "the only thing on my mind was getting into the 70s." He lowered his score to 74 in 1952, but rather than be satisfied, Nicklaus aimed for a new goal. "Now, of course, a paradise loomed: a round under 70."

*Even at age 13, Jack Nick-
laus had a near picture-
perfect swing.*

Father and son had always been close, but the time on the golf course further deepened their bonds. Nicklaus, who states that "I've never had a better friend" than his father, maintains that "my father's great gifts to me were his selfless-ness and the rocklike solidity of his character."

The older Nicklaus offered advice when asked and dished out warnings when needed. One day when Nicklaus was 11, the two stood on Scioto's 15th fairway. As Nicklaus related, "I had an 8-iron to the green. I put the shot in a bunker, and then I threw my club almost to the bunker. My father turned to me and said, very clearly, 'Young man, that will be the last club I'll ever see you throw or hear of you throwing, or you're not going to be playing this game.' I've never thrown a club since."

By the time he turned 12, Nicklaus had sur-passed his father's skill on the golf course. "I remember one day I hit as good a drive as I could, maybe 260 yards," recalled Louis Nicklaus. "I told Jack, 'If you outhit that one, I'll buy you a Cadillac convertible.' He hit his ball 25 or 30 yards past mine and I never outdrove him again."

Jack did not receive his Cadillac, but the booming shots indicated that he was ready to move into serious junior golf competition.

3

"GOLF IS WHAT I WANTED TO DO"

Nicklaus's steady play began to attract notice in golf circles, especially at Scioto Country Club, where he notched several rounds in the low 60s. One day his eighth grade teacher, Mrs. Helen Tanner, said in astonishment in class, "Why, Jack, I just looked in the paper this morning and they printed all the district handicaps and you're the lowest!"

The young golfer dominated junior golf in the Columbus area in 1953. He first captured the Ohio State Junior Championship for boys ages 13 to 15, then won the Columbus Junior Match Play Championship. That July, he even played a celebrity round in Columbus with the famous female golfer Patty Berg. For the first time, though, nerves overwhelmed Nicklaus, and he unleashed a series of embarrassing shots on his way to a horrendous 53 for nine holes.

Nicklaus would practice his putting until it got so dark he could hardly see the ball.

However, Nicklaus recovered in time to perform well in his first national tournament, the National Junior Championship held at Southern Hills in Tulsa, Oklahoma. Although he was the youngest out of 714 golfers entered in the contest, Nicklaus defeated three opponents before losing in the fourth round.

By now, some golf enthusiasts began comparing Nicklaus's feats with those of the legendary Bobby Jones, recognized as the greatest amateur ever to play the sport. Whether Jack deserved such praise while still so young might be questioned, but no one could doubt the teenager's commitment to excellence. He labored for hours on the practice tee to perfect his game. He later explained that a typical day in his early teens was "to go out in the morning in the summertime, hit golf balls for an hour or two, go play 18 holes, come in, have lunch, hit more golf balls, go out and play 18 more holes, come back in and hit more balls until dark."

Nicklaus practiced long after the other teenagers at Scioto had stored their clubs in the locker room. "I'd often putt well into the evening if there was enough moonlight to see the ball," and he hit so many balls on the practice range that his father moaned about the huge bill he had to pay each month. Claiming that the other teenagers at Scioto hit one or two buckets of balls, his father wondered, "You hit 10 buckets, a dozen buckets. How does anyone hit out that many?"

Club members became accustomed to seeing the blond-haired youth either on the practice range or the golf course. Even in winter, Nicklaus headed for the practice tee, where he boomed drive after drive from a heated shed, or he hiked out to one of the snow-clad fairways and cleared snow from a patch of grass so he could hit approach shots. "We never took vacations," explained Nicklaus. "I never went to camp as a kid. I played golf. That's what I wanted to do."

In 1955, Nicklaus first attracted attention at the national level by tying for first at the National Jaycees Juniors. Though he lost in a playoff, Nicklaus had now reached a level of play that few, if any, 15-year-olds could boast.

Being in the national spotlight carries its drawbacks, though. Later that summer Nicklaus headed to Richmond, Virginia, to play in the National Amateur, the most prestigious contest for the nation's amateur golfers. During a practice round, he cracked two mammoth shots to land on the 18th green, the only golfer to do this. Unknown to Nicklaus, Bobby Jones was watching from behind the green. When the second shot landed close to the pin, Jones asked a reporter who had hit such an impressive shot. When he learned that a 15-year-old had accomplished the feat, Jones stated he would like to meet the phenomenon.

"Young man," he said to Nicklaus, "I've heard that you're a very fine golfer. I'm coming out [to] watch you play a few holes tomorrow."

True to his word, Jones sat in his golf cart at 11 when Nicklaus walked up to hit his tee shot. Though he had played well to this point, the sight of his idol shook Nicklaus. "I was getting ready to drive off the eleventh tee when I saw Mr. Jones. I was one over par for 10 holes, but I became so excited, I hooked my drive into the woods. On the 12th, I skulled my approach over the green. On the 13th, I really blew. By then I was so nervous I could hardly hold the club. I felt miserable."

Nicklaus posted bogey, double bogey, bogey on those three holes and lost his match, but even worse was the sight of Bobby Jones leaving the gallery at 13. Nicklaus believed the famed amateur departed because of Nicklaus's poor play, but Jones had actually exited because he recognized his presence had rattled the young athlete.

Over the next two years, Nicklaus gained national recognition by capturing two important titles. He defeated Ohio's top professional and amateur golfers in the 1956 Ohio Open, during which he posted a first round 64. He followed that with his first national title by winning the 1957 U.S. Jaycees Junior Championship and its accompanying $1,000 college scholarship.

Despite the thousands of hours of practice he had put in, Nicklaus knew he lagged far behind most professionals. His fine play earned him a spot in the 1957 U.S. Open, the most prestigious of professional tournaments, but he missed advancing into the final two rounds of the four-round tournament by a whopping 10 shots. Then, after playing 18 holes with one of golf's all-time great professionals, Sam Snead, a humbled Nicklaus traveled home aware that, though he could drive as far as Snead, "when it came to iron play, I quickly realized I still had a great deal to learn about golf."

That's not to say he didn't have a lot of talent. In his first Professional Golf Association (PGA) tournament—the 1958 Rubber City Open held at the rugged Firestone Country Club in Akron, Ohio—Nicklaus stormed to the front after 36 holes with rounds of 67 and 66. However, when

When Jack Nicklaus became Ohio's all-around golf champion in 1956, he not only was the low amateur, but he also finished three strokes ahead of Earl Christiansen (right), the low pro.

he was paired in the third round with Art Wall and Tommy Bolt, two outstanding golfers who always drew huge crowds, nerves hampered the young golfer.

"The galleries were the largest I'd ever played in front of," mentioned Nicklaus, "and I was nervous as I could be." After flubbing six putts of less than three feet in the first nine holes, Nicklaus's round skyrocketed to a 76. Bolt advised Nicklaus to "just relax and enjoy yourself." Nicklaus listened, and he posted a final-round 68 to finish respectably in 12th place.

Not everything in Nicklaus's life revolved around golf. He was offered nearly 100 scholarships by different colleges, but Nicklaus enrolled at Ohio State University, where he joined a fra-

At age 19, Nicklaus was the youngest player in the British amateur championship. He was also the best as he won the title.

ternity and participated in intramural basketball, football, softball, volleyball, and tennis. Starting in the pre-pharmacy program, Nicklaus later changed his major to business administration, figuring that he might combine an insurance career with his amateur golf.

Nicklaus was trying to think more practically because now he had a wife to support. In his first week at the university, Nicklaus met Barbara Bash. They began going steady later that year, and after two years announced their engagement. On July 23, 1960, they were married at North Broadway Methodist Church in Columbus.

Nicklaus thought hard about whether he should turn professional. Only excellent golfers in those days made enough from the tour to support themselves, and only the top few got rich. Did he possess enough talent to earn the larger paychecks on the tour? He knew that at times he could hit a golf ball with the best, but he also realized that at crucial times in the past few years, his nerves had suffocated him. Could he contend with Snead, Bolt, Wall, and the popular Arnold Palmer? If not, he could always try to support a family by selling insurance while playing golf at the amateur level.

Nicklaus found his answer in the spring of 1959 when he was named to the nine-member Walker Cup team, a group of amateurs from the United States chosen to play in the historic Walker Cup Matches in Scotland against amateurs from Great Britain. Before these matches, Nicklaus questioned whether he had the skill to compete against top-flight golfers from his own nation, let alone the entire world. Being selected to such an elite team bolstered his self-confidence.

His play at the esteemed Muirfield course in Scotland, where he won both his matches and helped the United States team to victory, convinced Nicklaus that he belonged with golf's premier players. He stated afterward, "The goal of every amateur is to make the Walker Cup team. Simply being selected for it gave me a new confidence in myself. 'Here I am,' I told myself, 'playing right alongside these better players. I must be on a par with them.'"

When some athletes arrive at this realization, they stop doing what it was that got them to the top, but not Nicklaus. Rather than rest on his laurels, Nicklaus worked even harder. Now that he had reached one goal, he set a newer, loftier one—to continue to improve. "I began to demand much more of myself," explained Nicklaus, "and I began to play better than I ever had."

Immediately upon returning from Scotland, Nicklaus went on a tear. Over the next two years, he lost only once in 30 matches in capturing the North and South championship, the Grand Challenge Cup in England, and the Trans-Mississippi title. He topped those outstanding performances in September 1959, when he notched the first in a lengthy string of major championships in what would become admired by fellow golfers as typical Nicklaus style—pulling off the needed shot under extreme pressure. Nicklaus smoothly dropped a tricky eight-foot putt on the final hole to win the U.S. Amateur Championship by one stroke.

Nicklaus steamrolled through the 1960-61 amateur schedule as well, adding a Western Amateur championship and a second U. S. Amateur title to his ever-expanding list of victories. He grabbed everyone's attention at the 1960 World Amateur Team championship where he singlehandedly dismantled a tough Merion Golf Club in Pennsylvania with rounds of 66, 67, 68, 68. President Dwight D. Eisenhower, an avid golfer, met Nicklaus shortly afterward and enthused, "Mr. Nicklaus, at the Augusta National Golf Club, as you know, we build bridges to commemorate the records set by top players in the Masters. The way you're going, perhaps we should stop building those bridges. You look like you'll beat all the marks."

Nicklaus certainly displayed that talent at the 1960 U.S. Open, where he recorded a stellar 282—the lowest 72-hole total ever scored by an amateur in that prestigious event—and finished second to Arnold Palmer by two shots.

Actually, Nicklaus was somewhat disappointed with the result. With only six holes to play, he led the field by one shot, but a disappointing three-putt on 13, followed by another bogey at the next hole, dropped the amateur behind Palmer and the venerable, but shy, golfer Ben Hogan.

Afterward, Nicklaus explained that his awe of Ben Hogan, with whom he played, hurt him at the 13th green. When he looked at his second putt, an 18-inch tester, he saw that a poorly repaired ball mark that cut across his line might knock his ball off course, but he did not know if he could fix it. Afraid to ask the quiet Hogan whether he could repair it, and too embarrassed to show his ignorance of the rules by calling for an official, Nicklaus putted out. The ball veered off course when it rolled over the repair mark.

Though Hogan said few, if any, words during the entire round, he had plenty to say when reporters interviewed him later. Of his youthful partner, Hogan declared, "I played 36 holes today with a kid who should have won this thing by 10 strokes."

Nicklaus's string of steady performances settled the issue of whether he would remain an amateur or turn professional. Since he and Barbara wanted a large family, the money offered by the professional tour was hard to ignore. As he explained, "I just decided I wanted to play golf. And I owe it to my family to give them the best possible living I can."

Nicklaus had another reason for leaving the amateur ranks. He had long wanted to surpass golf records established by Bobby Jones. To do that, though, he had to compete with the best, and those men played on the professional tour. Thus, on November 8, 1961, the 21-year-old Nicklaus announced his decision to join the professional ranks. Golf would never be the same.

Arnold Palmer congratulates Nicklaus after the two finished one-two at the 1960 National Open in Denver. Nicklaus, still an amateur, beat all other players except Palmer.

4

"I REFUSED TO GET BEAT"

Nicklaus kicked off his career in unremarkable fashion by losing his initial event—an exhibition match against Gary Player—and by placing fiftieth at the 1962 Los Angeles Open, earning only $33.33. Labeled "The Golden Bear" by other professionals because of his blond hair and his heavyset frame, Nicklaus stormed through the next 16 tournaments. Though failing to take home a trophy, he placed second or third on five separate occasions, showing clearly that he belonged with the nation's top golfers.

His goals certainly placed him with the elite. He declared in 1962 that he wanted to become "the world's greatest golfer," and to do that he intended "to win more major championships than any other man. That is the true test. People 20 years from now won't be impressed that I earned $250,000 playing golf in one year."

Nicklaus realized that he had much to learn.

Arnold Palmer (in striped shirt at left) watches Nicklaus tee off at the 1962 World Series of Golf.

When he first appeared on tour, he carried one strategy for playing golf courses. "I just hit the ball as far as possible off the tee, found it, hit it onto the green, then hit it into the hole." The brash youth discovered that golf contained many more elements to master than distance, such as putting, chipping, and hitting intelligent shots. If he wanted to be considered the game's best, he had to improve in these areas.

"I've been thinking and working toward that goal ever since, and still see no end to the learning process, which for me is one of the factors that makes golf such a fascinating game."

Nicklaus entered the 1962 U. S. Open still looking for his first professional win. Held at Oakmont Country Club in Pennsylvania, the Open featured all the premier players, especially the current star, Arnold Palmer, who was more responsible than any man for popularizing golf. His good looks, zest for battle on the fairways, and brash charges breathed life into what many observers considered a stagnant game enjoyed only by the wealthy. Palmer's bold, almost reckless style captivated the nation, and wherever he appeared an enormous throng flooded to the course to watch him play. "Arnie's Army," as the crowd was called, embraced Palmer as its hero. Since Oakmont stood only minutes from Palmer's hometown of Latrobe, even larger numbers of boisterous supporters packed the course to cheer for their man.

Now, however, Arnie's Army had to put up with a challenger to the throne, and they turned their wrath upon this youth from Columbus. Nicklaus was everything Arnie's Army hated. Inexpressive during play, the opposite of Palmer with his frequent warm smiles, determined looks, and quickened steps, the machinelike Nicklaus attracted few fans. Galleries interpreted his lack of reaction as cold and unfeeling, whereas it simply was Nicklaus getting into his game.

"I get as nervous before and during a major tournament as anyone. But, I guess, it just doesn't show on me. I just can't help it if I don't show my feelings on the outside. If I don't set my jaw and jangle my change and tug at my hat, it doesn't mean I don't care. It's just my way."

The crewcut Nicklaus, pudgy at 5'11" and 210 pounds, also suffered in comparison to Palmer's dashing appearance. Women gave second and third looks to Palmer, while Nicklaus merely received a casual glance or two.

The worst offense Nicklaus committed, according to Arnie's Army, was that the young athlete had no fear of Palmer. As Nicklaus later stated, though he certainly respected Palmer's amazing talent, he was "another guy to beat on the road to where I wanted to go," an attitude that irritated Palmer's legions.

The stage was thus set for an incredible duel, should both golfers perform at the top of their games. They did. When the tournament ended on Sunday with Nicklaus and Palmer tied for first place, golf enthusiasts eagerly awaited the 18-hole playoff that would decide the champion.

Right away Nicklaus realized where the crowd's sympathy lay. Though Palmer had laughingly mentioned that, "I wish I were playing anybody but the big, strong, happy dude," his supporters held no such friendly feelings. Some ran and made noises as Nicklaus stood over putts. Others yelled out, "Miss it, Jack" when Nicklaus prepared to smack a drive or a fairway shot. Large signs appeared from the rough or out of bounds areas stating, "Over here, Fat Boy!" Though an embarrassed Palmer attempted to quiet the onlookers, they continued to behave in a boorish manner.

Nicklaus never let the crowd bother him. Instead, he focused on his game. "I never got scared. I just told myself not to be an idiot. When Palmer starts moving, most players get flustered and start making bogeys. I told myself to keep playing my own game—and I did."

Nicklaus vaulted to a four-shot lead after the first eight holes. Though Palmer mounted one of his patented charges and pulled to within one shot after 12, Nicklaus maintained his calm demeanor and won his first professional tournament—and major—with a three-stroke margin.

The Ohio golfer won three more events that season. For his accomplishments, he was named the PGA Tour's "Rookie of the Year" for 1962.

Though only a professional for one year, Nicklaus already displayed the qualities that made him a champion for four decades. Few athletes maintain such intense concentration as Nicklaus does, which he defines as "the ability to make my body do what my mind wants it to." He blocks out everything other than what needs to be done, whether in practice or during a tournament, and treats each shot as the most important one he will hit. Nicklaus never lets negative thoughts seep in. When he steps up to a drive or a fairway shot, he expects to pull off the type of shot he wants. One fellow professional mentioned that, "We're thinking what can go wrong with a shot rather than what should go right. His [Nicklaus's] mind is so permeated with the task at hand, there's no room for negatives."

Rather than simply hitting the ball, Nicklaus selects a precise place to direct the ball. On the tee, he selects "a target to hit rather than an area to avoid." When putting, his aim gets remarkably exact. "The difference between 'in' and 'almost' is all in the head. If you think the game is just a matter of getting it close and letting the law of averages do your work for you, you'll find a different way to miss every time. Your frame of reference must be exactly the width of the cup, not the general vicinity. When you're putting well, the only question is what part of the hole it's going to fall in, not if it's going in."

Thus during practice Nicklaus will play with only one ball, rather than hit two or three as many players frequently do. He knows that during a tournament, a golfer has to pull off pressure-packed shots with only one opportunity, and using a solitary ball during practice helps sharpen his ability to do that.

Louis Nicklaus watches his son chip onto the green at the 1962 U.S. Open.

Above all, Nicklaus loves playing when everything is at stake. Some athletes shy away from crucial occasions, but Nicklaus jumps at those chances.

"I do not like to lose. It's as simple as that," he explains. "Pride is probably my greatest motivation, because I just refuse to get beat, I can't stand to get beat, and I hate to have somebody come along and beat me."

Not that he had to worry about getting beat that often. In fact, by the mid-1960s, Nicklaus attained one of golf's most cherished achievements—winning all four major tournaments.

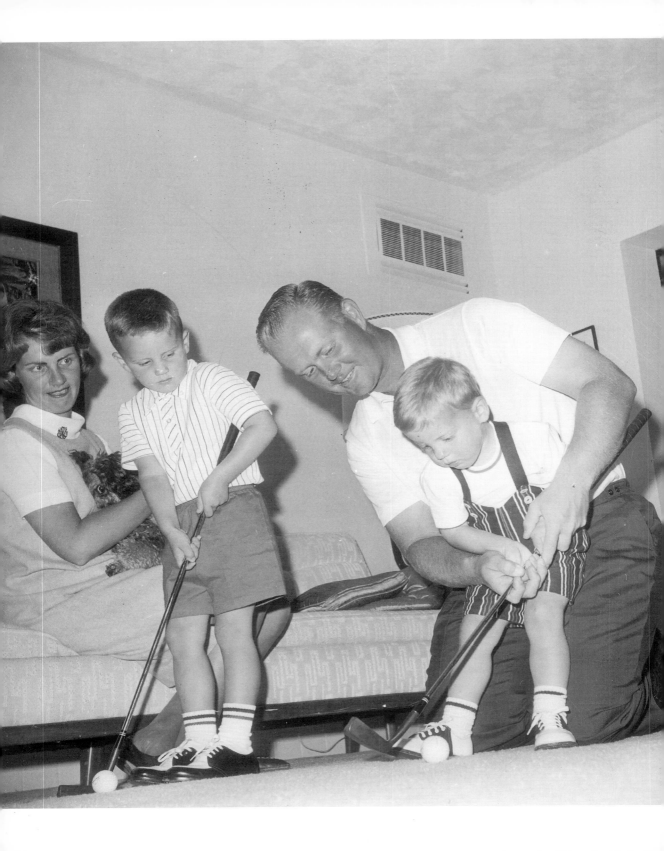

5

BREAKING BARRIERS

During the five-year span from 1962-1966, Nicklaus permanently stamped his name among golf's immortals by winning 21 PGA tour events, including six major titles. Most professionals battle to capture one or two championships of any type; to win one or two majors is a dream come true. Those numbers became an average year for Nicklaus in his prime.

After his initial major championship in the 1962 U.S. Open, Nicklaus added the Masters and PGA championships in 1963, the Masters in 1964, and a third Masters in 1965 as well as his first British Open. Before his 27th birthday, Nicklaus had matched feats with the best to play the sport. Bobby Jones gushed after Nicklaus shattered the Masters' scoring record in 1965 that, "Jack is playing an entirely different game—a game with which I am not familiar."

Though Nicklaus tallied victories in speedy

Jack Nicklaus gives golf lessons to sons Jackie (left) and Steve while wife Barbara and French poodle Nappy look on.

fashion, he would not place himself with Jones, Snead, or Hogan until he won all four of the major titles. After compiling three of the four in only two full years on tour, Nicklaus failed to capture the final major—the British Open—four years in a row. A determined Nicklaus flew to Scotland for the 1966 British Open intent on completing his quartet of majors.

Nicklaus arrived at Muirfield, located 20 miles east of Edinburgh along Scotland's eastern coast, one week early so he could play additional practice rounds to learn the course. He immediately noticed that British golf authorities had altered the ancient Muirfield tract by allowing the rough to grow unchecked and by drastically narrowing fairways. One golf writer even noted that, "I have never seen such tall rough, for the flowering spears of bent grass, going to seed, stood well over a foot high and actually waved in the wind like a field of wheat."

These changes placed a premium on accurate shot making and penalized the long hitter. It would not be enough to simply smash drive after drive as far as possible, for if a ball veered even a tiny amount off course, it would land in the thick rough. To win this tournament, a golfer would have to hit shorter, more controlled shots that kept his ball in the fairways, so Nicklaus decided to avoid using his driver on most holes. As one of the game's longest hitters, he surrendered one of his strengths before the tournament even started.

Nicklaus turned what appeared to be a negative factor into a positive one. "Instead of deciding to hate the new Muirfield, I made up my mind on that first walk around that I would just have

to accommodate myself to it." Rather than trying to hammer the course into submission with his normal game, Nicklaus adapted to the course.

The tactic worked. After two rounds Nicklaus led the field with scores of 70 and 67. He stumbled badly in the third round by bogeying four of the final holes, allowing Phil Rodgers to close a nine-shot deficit in as many holes to sweep past Nicklaus by two shots. Few players could lose nine shots to a rival and still maintain enough composure to battle back.

Nicklaus was not any player. Paired with Rodgers in the final round, Nicklaus tallied three birdies in the front nine to jump back into the lead. Two subsequent bogeys dropped him into a tie with Dave Thomas and Doug Sanders, and by the time Nicklaus walked to the 17th tee, he

Both Jack Nicklaus and his caddie celebrate a birdie on the 15th hole of the 1966 Masters. The putt helped stave off hard-charging Tommy Jacobs and won the tournament for Nicklaus.

In a tune-up for the British Open, Nicklaus (right) teamed up with Gary Player (left) to defeat teenage stars Bobby Cole (second from left) and Peter Townsend (second from right).

knew he needed one birdie and a par to clinch his victory.

Even though the 17th hole was a long par-5, Nicklaus resisted the temptation to pull out his driver and go for distance. Instead, he cracked a 3-iron 280 yards down the middle of the fairway, then dropped a 5-iron 15 feet from the hole.

"I saw it land on the fairway about 15 feet short of the green," recalled Nicklaus, "and then—it seemed an awful long time later—a loud roar went up from the gallery packed around the green." After grabbing his birdie with two putts, Nicklaus faced only the long par-4 18th hole.

Again, he split the fairway with a 1-iron, then

smacked a 3-iron to within 25 feet of the pin. When he tapped in his second putt for the victory, Nicklaus became only the fourth player in golf's history to win all four majors.

This tournament showed that Nicklaus possessed more than simply a long game. Though a young professional, he acted with the calm composure of a veteran by refusing to use his driver. He had the mental toughness to stick to a game plan, outlast rivals, and hold on when victory seemed to be slipping away. As one writer stated afterward, "Nicklaus's ultimate victory was as much a triumph of character as of golfing ability."

Though golf is Nicklaus's business, he never lets it get in the way of what he considers his most important responsibility—his duties as a husband and father. Mainly out of concern for their children, Barbara and he moved to North Palm Beach, Florida, in 1965. Though at first planning only to winter there, the couple made it their permanent home so that the children would not have to change schools in mid-year. As Nicklaus explained, "We wanted our kids to be able to grow up right—in one place, with one set of friends, rather than having to shift from one school to another each year."

While most professional golfers play in 30 or more tournaments every year, Nicklaus averaged 20 so he would not have to be away from Barbara and their five children—Jack Jr., Steven, Nancy Jean, Gary, and Michael—too often. Nicklaus holds to a rule to "never be away from home more than 14 straight days. Golf has been a great and rewarding thing in my life, but it's not everything and never will be." Fellow golfer and close friend Chi Chi Rodriguez once said, only half jokingly, that "Jack Nicklaus is a legend in his spare time."

Nicklaus rarely missed one of his sons' or daughter's school events, even in the busiest of years. After winning one U.S. Open title, he caught an overnight flight home so that he could attend Steven's baseball game the next day. In a two-year stretch, he missed only four of Jack and Steven's football and basketball games.

Whenever possible, Nicklaus organized all-day competitions with his sons, their neighborhood friends, and the athletic director of the local junior high school. These nine-event contests included golf, tennis, Ping-Pong, one-on-one basketball, free throw shooting, pool, punt-pass-kick, swimming, and a 40-yard dash. "You should have seen those two fathers trying as hard as they could to beat the kids," laughed Barbara. "They think they're still all-round athletes anyway."

Only one worry concerned Nicklaus as the 1960s closed. Through the early years on tour his weight—which wavered between 210-215—never affected him, even though he disliked the various nicknames that came with it. Classmates at Ohio State labeled him "Whaleman," "Blobbo," and "Jelly," while tour golfers pinned the name "Ohio Fats" to the young athlete when he joined their ranks.

However, during the 1969 Ryder Cup matches in England, Nicklaus weakened near the end of some of his contests. "I was getting tired and knew it was time to act." On the plane trip back home, he told Barbara that he intended to shed the extra weight.

Nicklaus attacked his new goal with the same

intensity that he approached golf. In five weeks he slimmed down to 190 and altered his old-style crew cut to a fresher look. When Nicklaus appeared for his first tournament in 1970, his new look not only stunned fellow professionals, but also suddenly made him an attractive spokesman for a wide variety of products.

"Nobody likes to be called fat or a slob," asserted Nicklaus. "I never liked reading such things about myself." With typical dedication, he embarked upon a rigid diet where he followed one day of eating anything he wanted with two or three days of tuna fish, broccoli, and other healthy foods.

In his first eight years, Nicklaus rose to the top of almost everybody's list of great golfers. He won 32 tour events by the end of 1969, including seven major tournaments—totals that most professionals could accomplish only in their dreams. Though he now entered the 1970s, Nicklaus was far from finished.

"The way it seems to me, in golf you're always breaking a barrier. When you bust it, you set yourself a little higher barrier and try to break that one."

6

"NICKLAUS NEVER STOPS TRYING"

Break barriers is precisely what Nicklaus did. In 1970, at the renowned Old Course at historic St. Andrews in Scotland, the birthplace of golf, Nicklaus snatched his second British Open from the hands of a surprised Doug Sanders by clinching an 18-hole playoff on the final hole. As Sanders looked on, confident of heading to sudden death, Nicklaus drained an eight-foot birdie putt for the victory.

When he followed that the next year by capturing the PGA Championship, Nicklaus became the first golfer to ever win each major twice. Two years later he passed a record some had deemed untouchable—Bobby Jones's 13 victories in major tournaments. Nicklaus's second PGA Championship in three years raised his total of major titles to 14, placing him squarely at the forefront of his sport.

Unanimously, fellow professionals and golf

Nicklaus has great powers of concentration. Here he lines up a putt at a 1972 tournament.

49

observers hailed him as the finest to play the game. For his abilities, he was named the PGA Player of the Year in 1972, 1973, 1975, and 1976 and *Sports Illustrated's* "Athlete of the Decade" for the 1970s.

Nicklaus did not confine his business pursuits to simply playing golf. During the 1970s, he started Golden Bear International, Inc., a diverse concern that manufactures golf products. He took an active hand in running the business, especially the golf architecture branch, where he could help design new golf courses. In typical fashion, Nicklaus learned everything he could about the maintenance of plants, flowers, and various strains of grass.

As his tournament schedule slowed, Nicklaus devoted more time to building Golden Bear International, which he found almost as challenging as his golf. He loved sitting down with top advisors to chart the company's future, and he felt energized by the "discussions, the decision-making, the problem-solving, the need to use your brain."

However, he did not allow family time to suffer. His typical workweek when home would be two full days and three half days at the office, thereby freeing the afternoons for his family, fishing, or a friendly game of golf.

Now that he reigned as golf's king, in the mid-1970s Nicklaus had to fend off a series of challengers who had designs on replacing him. Two of the best were a fellow golfer from Ohio State, Tom Weiskopf, and another golden-haired young professional named Johnny Miller.

The three had a showdown at the 1975 Masters, where they switched positions on the leader board through much of the tournament. On

Augusta's final three holes, Miller and Weiskopf missed easy birdie putts that would have lifted them into the lead, while Nicklaus again proved his toughness under pressure by sinking a winding, lightning-quick birdie putt from 40 feet away to win the tournament.

His main competitor, however, came out of Stanford University. Tom Watson stood at the head of a stellar group of challengers that included not only Weiskopf and Miller, but also Lee Trevino. He opened the friendly rivalry with Nicklaus by snatching the 1977 Masters away from Nicklaus with a late birdie. At that year's British Open, played at Turnberry, Watson and Nicklaus met again and put on a display of head-to-head golf rarely seen before.

At the tournament's halfway point, Nicklaus, Watson, Trevino, and Hubert Green stood one shot behind the leader, Roger Maltbie. Paired together for the third round, Nicklaus and Watson played such outstanding golf that they left the other competitors far behind and turned the contest into a two-man show.

After nine holes of the third round, Nicklaus opened a two-shot advantage over Watson, but the Stanford athlete answered with a birdie barrage of his own on the back nine to pull even. Each man had posted a 65 while other golfers struggled to shoot 70.

Together again for the final round, neither man gave an inch. Though Watson seemed to play better than his rival, Nicklaus's unparalleled ability to pull off incredible shots or sink long putts had the two bouncing in and out of the lead. Nicklaus rushed to a three-stroke lead by the fourth hole, but three Watson birdies over the next four holes brought him even with 10

*Nicklaus chips out of the
woods at the 1972 Masters.*

holes remaining.

Nicklaus followed a Watson bogey
at the ninth by birdieing the twelfth
for a two-shot advantage, but again
Watson responded with birdies at
13 and 15. With only three holes
left, the two stood dead even again.

Both parred the 16th. On the
17th green, Nicklaus faltered and
missed a short putt. Now one shot
behind Watson, Nicklaus knew he
had to birdie the final hole to have
any chance of winning the Open.

The 18th at Turnberry, a 431-
yard par 4, presented a difficult
challenge. When Nicklaus pushed
his drive far to the right in deep
rough, only inches from the base
of a bush and underneath a low-
hanging branch, the gallery all but
conceded the match to Watson. No
one standing in the vicinity gave
Nicklaus even a slight chance of advancing his
ball very far, let alone knocking it onto the green.
Matters worsened moments later when Watson
drilled a beautiful 7-iron two feet from the flag.
Nicklaus's only chance was to somehow power
his ball out of the deep rough onto the green,
sink his putt, and hope that Watson missed his
simple putt.

Forced to shorten his swing because of the
branch, Nicklaus summoned every ounce of
strength, hacked down with an 8-iron directly
through the branch, and somehow hit the ball
squarely. It darted into the air and landed 35
feet from the hole.

Though he pulled off one miraculous shot, he

still had to drop the long putt. After carefully examining it from every angle, Nicklaus rammed the ball home. Moments later, though, Watson ended Nicklaus's brief hope by sinking his own short putt for the title.

The two stunned the golf world with their play over the final two days. Nicklaus recorded only one bogey to post scores of 65 and 66, but lost to Watson's successive 65s. Each man shattered the British Open record for lowest score and had so far distanced themselves from the rest of the field that the third-place finisher, Hubert Green, stood 11 shots back. Watson tallied his total with steady golf, while Nicklaus repeatedly pulled out of perilous situations with spectacular recovery shots, accurate putting, and a gritty determination to never give up.

"I cannot remember a head-to-head battle that can begin to compare with the one Nicklaus and Watson waged two days running," gushed one golf observer. "No matter what the odds are, Nicklaus never stops fighting, and you never know when he will contrive some small miracle like that impossible three on the last hole."

Nicklaus had lost two major tournaments to Watson by a total of two strokes, but no one was yet ready to hand Nicklaus's crown to the Stanford challenger. In fact, the Golden Bear still had plenty of fight left in him.

7

"GIVE IT EVERYTHING I'VE GOT"

He had his doubters, though, as the 1980s arrived. He performed so miserably at both the 1979 U.S. and British Opens that he failed to qualify for weekend play. He did not win a single tournament in 1979, and he began 1980 in equally dismal fashion. In the first seven events he entered, he missed three cuts, withdrew from a fourth, and won a mere $4,404 in the other three. Murmurs could be heard that brought up the question of his retirement, a topic that would have been unthinkable one year earlier.

Nicklaus did not believe his playing career was finished. Besides, he could not even think of retiring while playing so poorly. To ensure he did not end his spectacular career in horrendous fashion, Nicklaus practiced even harder than before. "I want to make sure that each year that I play I give it everything I've got."

Nicklaus blasts out of a trap at the 1980 U.S. Open held in Springfield, New Jersey. It would be the last major tournament he would win until his historic comeback at the 1986 Masters.

When Nicklaus sets his mind on something, results usually follow in rapid time. Though he later admitted that "I've wondered for the last year and a half if I should still be playing this silly game," he served notice that the Golden Bear was far from hibernating. In June 1980, he shredded the difficult Baltusrol Golf Course for an opening round 63 in the U.S. Open. Nicklaus fans in the gallery the next day wore T-shirts proclaiming, "Jack is Back," and they enthusiastically cheered his every shot over the next three days as he outdueled Japan's Isao Aoki for a two-shot victory in yet another major tournament.

Two years later he again battled Tom Watson in a memorable finish to another U.S. Open. Held over the breathtaking—and arduous—Pebble Beach course in California, which Nicklaus has always listed as his favorite golf course, he and Watson shared the lead with two holes remaining. However, Watson pulled off one of golf's greatest shots when he sank a chip from deep rough behind the 17th green to claim the title. Though Nicklaus had lost one more time to Watson, he certainly illustrated that he remained a dominant force.

Though disappointed, Nicklaus also proved his grace under defeat. After Watson completed the 18th hole, Nicklaus was there with outstretched hand to congratulate him. "You little son of a gun," he grinned at Watson, "you're something else. That was nice going. I'm really proud of you, and I'm pleased for you."

Nicklaus's sportsmanship here, and throughout his career, showed what a true champion he was. Good manners and cheerfulness are simple in victorious moments, but Nicklaus made a point to never complain about losing to another gifted golfer. One observer who had long covered Nicklaus's career wrote that, "As far as I can see, Nicklaus is the best loser in sports. I have never heard him offer an excuse for not winning."

Two years later, when Nicklaus won the emotional 1986 Masters, the editors of *Golf Magazine*, to celebrate the 100th anniversary of golf in the United States, listed their "100 Heroes of Golf." At a New York dinner, before 34 other golf greats, including Ben Hogan and Arnold Palmer, Nicklaus received the coveted "Player of the Century" award in recognition of his outstanding record and contributions to the game. Though such an award can cause jealousy or criticism, no one debated the selection.

In January 1990, Nicklaus turned 50 and moved on to the next stage of his career—the Senior Tour. Consisting strictly of players age 50 and above, the Senior Tour captivated audiences who poured onto golf courses for another opportunity to watch golf greats compete against one another. As he did on the regular tour, Nicklaus dominated play, particularly in those tournaments considered majors—the Senior U.S. Open, The PGA Seniors' Championship, The Tradition, and the Senior Players Championship. By 1996, Nicklaus had won eight of the 32 events he entered, and seven of those titles were in the majors.

When one examines the records of golf's greatest, none can compare and few come close to Nicklaus's achievements. The only man to win championships in five different decades, Nicklaus set the standard for greatness by capturing 20 major tournaments while an amateur and

JACK NICKLAUS

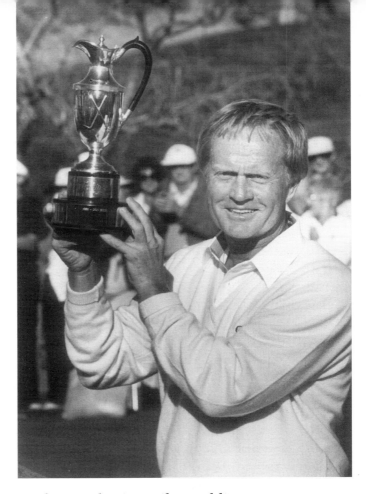

Nicklaus shows off the trophy he won at the 1990 Tradition golf tournament. It was the first senior tournament he was eligible to play in.

on the regular tour, then adding seven more on the Senior Tour. In his heyday, from 1962-1979, Nicklaus placed in the top 10 in almost 70% of the 357 tournaments he entered, and increased that to over 80% of the tournaments as a Senior. To honor his spectacular career, Nicklaus was inducted into the World Golf Hall of Fame.

While tournament play has diminished for Nicklaus, other aspects of golf have increased. His Golden Bear International prospers, and Nicklaus has devoted more time to golf architecture, creating such beautiful layouts as Glen Abbey Golf Club near Toronto, Canada, and the Muirfield Village Golf Course near Columbus,

Ohio, where, each year since 1976, he has hosted his own tournament, the Memorial. While proud of his deeds on the golf course, Nicklaus realizes that life does not exist solely for work or career acclaim. He loves following the paths chosen by his sons and daughter, with whom he and Barbara are very close, and frequently directs his comments in interviews to teenagers.

"I think that whatever you do," Nicklaus replied to a question asking what he would say to teenagers about how they can succeed, "you should do it to the best of your ability and you should have fun doing it. If you don't enjoy it, it's not going to be good and you're not going to be successful at it.

"Also, you should set goals that are higher than you think you can achieve. Too often, people set goals that are too low, and they don't accomplish as much. If you set lofty goals, then even if you don't reach all the way, you'll still achieve far more than if you set lower goals."

Those words, intended for young people, form an accurate description of his own remarkable life.

CHRONOLOGY

1940   Born in Columbus, Ohio, on January 21.

1953   Wins Ohio State Junior Championship and the Columbus Junior Match Play Championship.

1957   Wins his first national title, the U.S. Jaycees Junior Championship.

1959   Wins first U.S. Amateur Championship.

1960   Repeats as U.S. Amateur Champion; comes in second overall and low amateur at the U.S. Open.

1962   Wins first pro tournament—the U.S. Open in a thrilling playoff against Arnold Palmer; is named Rookie of the Year.

1965   Wins his third Masters in a row and first British Open.

1971   Becomes first golfer ever to win each major tournament twice.

1973   Surpasses Bobby Jones's record of 13 major victories.

1986   Wins Masters in one of the greatest comebacks in all of sports history; is named Player of the Century.

1996   Wins his seventh major senior title.

STATISTICS

NUMBER OF VICTORIES EACH YEAR

Year	Victories	Year	Victories	Year	Victories
1962	3	1974	2	1985	0
1963	5	1975	5	1986	1
1964	4	1976	2	1987	0
1965	5	1977	3	1988	0
1966	3	1978	4	1989	0
1967	5	1979	0	1990	2
1968	2	1980	2	1991	3
1969	3	1981	0	1992	0
1970	3	1982	1	1993	1
1971	5	1983	0	1994	1
1972	7	1984	1	1995	1
1973	7				

MAJOR VICTORIES ON THE PGA TOUR

U.S. Open	1962, 1967, 1972, 1980
Masters	1963, 1965, 1966, 1972, 1975, 1986
PGA	1963, 1971, 1973, 1975, 1980
British Open	1966, 1970, 1978

ABOUT THE AUTHOR

John F. Wukovits is a teacher and writer from Trenton, Michigan, who specializes in sports, the Wild West, and World War II history. His work has appeared in more than 25 publications, including *PGA Magazine* and *Sports History*. His earlier books include a biography of World War II admiral Clifton Sprague, and several Chelsea House biographies of people such as Barry Sanders, Vince Lombardi, and Jesse James. A graduate of the University of Notre Dame, Wukovits is the father of three daughters—Amy, Julie, and Karen.

FURTHER READING

Alliss, Peter. *Peter Alliss's Supreme Champions of Golf.* New York: Charles Scribner's Sons, 1986.

Associated Press Sports Staff. *The Sports Immortals.* Englewood Cliffs, New Jersey: Prentice-Hall, Inc., 1972.

Bonventre, Peter. *Neil Leifer's Sports Stars.* Garden City, New York: Doubleday & Company, Inc., 1985.

Boswell, Thomas. *Strokes of Genius.* Garden City, New York: Doubleday & Company, Inc., 1987.

Bryan, Mike. *Dogleg Madness.* New York: The Atlantic Monthly Press, 1988.

Editors of Salem Press. *Great Athletes: The Twentieth Century.* Englewood Cliffs, New Jersey: Salem Press, 1992.

Hobbs, Michael. *Great Opens: Historic British and American Championships 1913-1975.* New York: A. S. Barnes and Company, 1976.

Klein, Dave. *Great Moments in Golf.* New York: Cowles Book Company, Inc., 1971.

Nicklaus, Jack with Herbert Warren Wind. *The Greatest Game of All: My Life in Golf.* New York: Simon & Schuster, 1969.

Nicklaus, Jack with Ken Bowden. *On and Off the Fairway: A Pictorial Autobiography.* New York: Simon & Schuster, 1978.

Peper, George, with Robin McMillan and James A. Frank. *Golf in America: The First One Hundred Years.* New York: Harry N. Abrams, Inc., 1988.

Seitz, Nick. *Superstars of Golf.* New York: Golf Digest, Inc., 1978.

Wind, Herbert Warren. *Following Through.* New York: Ticknor & Fields, 1985.

INDEX

PHOTO CREDITS:
UPI/Corbis-Bettmann: 2, 52; AP/Wide World Photos: 6, 9, 29, 30, 33, 34, 40, 44, 54, 58; Corbis-Bettmann: 12, 16, 39, 43, 48; reprinted with permission of Columbus (OH) Post-Dispatch: 18, 22, 24.